THE
TIMING
of GOD

His Timetable *for* Your Life

Parsons Publishing House
Melbourne, Florida USA

THE TIMING OF GOD: His Timetable for Your Life
by Ed King

Parsons Publishing House
P. O. Box 410063
Melbourne, FL 32941 USA
www.ParsonsPublishingHouse.com
Info@ParsonsPublishingHouse.com

This book or parts thereof may not be reproduced in any form, stored in a retrieval system, or transmitted in any form by any means⊠electronic, mechanical, photocopy, recording or otherwise⊠without prior written permission of the publisher, except as provided by the United States copyright law.

All Scripture quotations, unless otherwise indicated, are taken from the *Holy Bible, King James Version* (Public Domain). Scripture quotations marked (NIV) are taken from the *Holy Bible, New International Version*®, NIV®. Copyright © 1973, 1978, 1984 by Biblica, Inc.™ Used by permission of Zondervan. All rights reserved worldwide. www.zondervan.com. Scripture quotations marked (AMP) are taken from the *Amplified® Bible*. Copyright © 1954, 1958, 1962, 1964, 1965, 1987 by The Lockman Foundation. Used by permission.

Copyright © 2021, 2016 by Ed King
All rights reserved.

ISBN -13: 978-1-60273-071-7
ISBN -10: 1-60273-071-7
Library of Congress Control Number: 2016915854
First edition publishied 2016. Second edition 2021.
Printed in the United States of America.
For World-Wide Distribution.

TABLE OF CONTENTS

	Introduction	v
1	It's All About Timing	1
2	A Time to Decrease	5
3	A Time to Learn	7
4	An Appointed Time	13
5	Timing in God's Kingdom	17
6	God's Blessing	19
7	God's Divine Timetable	23
8	How to Miss the Will of God	27
9	Times & Seasons	33
10	Willing & Obedient	37
11	He Cares for Us	39
12	Let God Judge	43
13	Focused on Him	47
14	A Time to Mature	51
15	Promoting the Kingdom	55
16	A Time to Prepare	61
17	A Time for Action	67
18	Responsible Living	71
19	God Will Develop You	77
20	Faithful to Your Call	85
21	Persevere to the End	91
22	Finish Strong	97
	About the Author	101

THE TIMING OF GOD

Introduction

Jesus is the greatest example of a person who was totally committed to following God's precise timetable for His life. He never tried to circumvent God's perfect plan by doing things the way He wanted and when He wanted. Jesus was confident in His heavenly Father's timetable.

God has established a heavenly timetable for your life as well. There is an opportune time for each one of us to do certain things. There is a time to educate ourselves, and there is a time to put that education to work. There is a time to prepare for ministry, and then there is a time to minister. We, like Jesus, need to be totally committed to God's perfect timing for our lives. Just as parents are aware that their children are unable to respond beyond their level of maturity, God is aware of the same thing for His children. There is a time to crawl, a time to walk, and then a time to run the race to its fullest.

Timing is everything. Many Christians get into trouble more often than not by moving out ahead of the timing of God, not because of a misguided heart or even a failure to hear from Him. We must have confidence in our heavenly Father and trust that He knows the perfect timing for our lives.

CHAPTER 1

It's All About Timing

The ability to discern and then operate in God's timing concerning your life is one of the most important lessons you will ever learn. In the next several pages, you will see that everything has a time and a season. God wants to give you wonderful things to enjoy, but He will give them to you when the time is right—in His time.

Jesus—Our Example

> These words spake Jesus, and lifted up his eyes to heaven, and said, Father, **the hour is come**; glorify thy Son, that thy Son also may glorify thee: (John 17:1, emphasis added).

THE TIMING OF GOD

Although there is quite a bit that could be said about this verse, the main point is this: Jesus said to His Father, "The hour is come." We need to understand the importance of that phrase, not merely gloss over it, failing to realize the importance of what Jesus is actually saying. He said that there was a specific time for things to happen, and that time has come.

Jesus knew the importance of timing as it relates to God's Kingdom and how vital it is to all of us. Timing is critical. Timing is everything.

Notice that Jesus said to His Father, "The hour is come, glorify Thy Son." In other words, there was a specific time when Jesus was to be glorified and be lifted up. He goes on to say, "Glorify thy Son, that thy Son may also glorify thee." When the Son was glorified, the Father was exalted or glorified also. The exaltation of the Son of God brings exaltation and glorification of the heavenly Father, as well.

> "From that **time** Jesus began to preach, and to say, Repent: for the kingdom of heaven is at hand" (Matthew 4:17, emphasis added).

You'll need to understand the setting in which this verse was spoken so that you can begin to appreciate the events that led up to it. Let's go back to the first verse of the same chapter and carry on from there.

> Then was Jesus led up of the Spirit into the wilderness to be tempted of the devil. And when he had fasted forty days and forty nights, he was

It's All About Timing

afterward an hungred. And when the tempter came to him, he said, If thou be the Son of God, command that these stones be made bread. But he answered and said, It is written, Man shall not live by bread alone, but by every word that proceedeth out of the mouth of God. Then the devil taketh him up into the holy city, and setteth him on a pinnacle of the temple, And saith unto him, If thou be the Son of God, cast thyself down: for it is written, He shall give his angels charge concerning thee: and in their hands they shall bear thee up, lest at any time thou dash thy foot against a stone. Jesus said unto him, It is written again, Thou shalt not tempt the Lord thy God. Again, the devil taketh him up into an exceeding high mountain, and sheweth him all the kingdoms of the world, and the glory of them; And saith unto him, All these things will I give thee, if thou wilt fall down and worship me. Then saith Jesus unto him, Get thee hence, Satan: for it is written, Thou shalt worship the Lord thy God, and him only shalt thou serve. Then the devil leaveth him, and, behold, angels came and ministered unto him (Matthew 4:1-11).

These verses in Matthew tell us that Jesus was led into the wilderness by the Spirit of God to be tempted by the devil. He fasted and prayed for forty days and forty nights while satan relentlessly tempted Him with every temptation known to mankind: the lusts of the flesh, the lust of the eye, and the pride of life—these are the things that all of life eventually boils down to. Satan tempted Jesus spiritually, emotionally (or soulishly), and physically. He tempted Him spirit, soul, and body, and Jesus overcame them all.

CHAPTER 2

A Time to Decrease

The Gospel of the apostle John records another man named John—John, the Baptist—speaking of Jesus, "He must increase, but I must decrease" (John 3:30).

John the Baptist was quite aware of the specific, but temporary, span of time that his ministry was to occupy. His job was highly focused and resolute; he was preparing the way of the Lord. He knew there was a definite beginning and end to his efforts.

Likewise, we must also decrease, but Jesus will always increase. Our influence on the Earth is for a relatively short span of time and then it ceases. Although temporary, we can perpetuate our influence and cause it to persevere by building a work—a ministry for God—that will consistently bear fruit whether we are physically there or not. For example, I am the founding pastor of Redemption Church in Knoxville, Tennessee. If, for some reason I were to be temporarily called away, there would still be a great deal of fruit remaining behind—a substantial amount of ministry taking place in my absence. Jesus' influence around the world will always increase and altogether more as the body of Christ jointly promotes Him.

Transition at the Right Time

> "From that **time** Jesus began to preach, and to say, Repent: for the kingdom of heaven is at hand" (Matthew 4:17, emphasis added).

Looking at chapter four in Matthew, we see God's timing emphasized. This verse conveys to us the idea that for Jesus to remain in God's will, He could not start preaching before a designated point in time. John the Baptist had been preaching tirelessly to help prepare the way for the Messiah's arrival. Jesus had to wait for John the Baptist's ministry to come to fruition before He could take over and begin preaching His message, "The kingdom of heaven is at hand." The Lord could not have preached it, however, before the time was right—before God was ready.

We need to carefully follow the example that Jesus laid out before us. He did not get out ahead of God or begin anything before God gave Him permission to proceed. Jesus began both to preach and begin His ministry at a specific time.

CHAPTER 3

A Time to Learn

Why did Jesus come into this Earth the way He did? He could have just as easily come into the Earth preaching the Word. He could have done anything He wanted, but He chose to go through the process of maturing and qualifying Himself—identifying with humanity by taking the time to learn about us by walking in our shoes. Being God, He obviously knew us, but He knew us from a different point of view.

For instance, I may know a great deal about the people of Africa from a strictly scholastic point of view, but I will never know what it is truly like to be a true African man. I will never know how the environment in which he grew up influenced his decision-making, social skills, education, and his view of the world. To truly understand all the nuances involved, I would have to be born an African.

Because Jesus was born into the Earth from a woman and grew up associating with friends, neighbors, and clients from His carpentry business, He effectively upended any notion of any inability to effectively identify with humanity. Jesus totally identified with you in everything He did; He was a man and is still a man today. The fact that He is still a man is harder for some people to accept than the fact that He was a man when He started. There was one mediator between God and man—**the man**, Christ Jesus. He lives today as a man—a God-man.

A Time to Reveal

There was a specific time when Jesus began to preach. He waited to begin His ministry until after God gave Him permission. There was nothing premature about His actions.

> When Jesus came into the coasts of Caesarea Philippi, he asked his disciples, saying, Whom do men say that I the Son of man am? And they said, Some say that thou art John the Baptist: some, Elias; and others, Jeremias, or one of the prophets. He saith unto them, But whom say ye that I am? And Simon Peter answered and said, Thou art the Christ, the Son of the living God (Matthew 16:13-16).

Simon Peter was correct, but you must understand something about Jesus up to that point: He had not given any of His disciples a single clue as to His true identity. I hear you saying, "Oh, come on, Jesus had surely told them that He was the Son of the Living God." Sorry. Not a chance. He did not tell them anything about who He was until Simon Peter stated it back in verse sixteen. Let's single out that verse and look at it again.

> And Jesus answered and said unto him, Blessed art thou, Simon Barjona: for flesh and blood hath not revealed it unto thee, but my Father which is in heaven (Matthew 16:17).

Jesus did not tell him, and man did not reveal it to him. It was revelation knowledge; the supernatural realm was revealing something to Peter. Moreover, God called Simon Peter blessed because he received that supernatural revelation from God.

You need to understand why this is so important. Jesus said many times in the Bible that He only wanted to do the things He saw His Father do—within God's timetable. Jesus was waiting on the Father's timing to reveal His identity to His disciples; He was unwavering—knowing that in God's perfect timing it was all planned beforehand.

Talk about patience! Talk about endurance! Talk about discipline! Jesus knew who He was; He knew that He had come to set humanity free. He knew He was the Christ, Son of the living God. Even so, He did not open His mouth and teach the disciples anything about His life and ministry until the Father revealed it to Simon Peter.

> And I say also unto thee, That thou art Peter, and upon this rock I will build my church; and

> the gates of hell shall not prevail against it. And I will give unto thee the keys of the kingdom of heaven: and whatsoever thou shalt bind on earth shall be bound in heaven: and whatsoever thou shalt loose on earth shall be loosed in heaven. Then charged he his disciples that they should tell no man that he was Jesus the Christ (Matthew 16:18-20).

Jesus urged His disciples not to tell anyone that He was the Christ. He specifically told them not to go out and spread it all over town because Jesus knew that many problems would possibly arise making ministry more difficult. Jesus also told a couple of other people whom He had healed to keep their results quiet, but His words—forgive me—fell on deaf ears, so to speak. Jesus also urged a man that He healed of blindness to keep silent about his miracle, but almost immediately, the man went out and told everyone who would listen about the great miracle of sight he had received from the Lord. From that moment on, Jesus had no privacy or peace. It wasn't that Jesus didn't want him to testify of God's goodness; the problem was that the timing wasn't yet expedient for God's purposes.

Think back over your life. Has Jesus ever told you something and told you not to tell anyone? Certainly, He has. Over the course of your life, God will disclose many things to you that need not be revealed to anyone else. However, if you persist in your quest to disobey God by telling people all the wonderful things He has shown you; you probably will not be bothered much longer with Him showing you anything at all. He did not show you those things so you could impress your friends; He showed you because He wanted to reveal something just to you—from Dad to His son or daughter. There could come a time where God might ask you to reveal those things to others, but generally, it's probably just information for you alone.

Building a Foundation

> From that time forth began Jesus to shew unto his disciples, how that he must go unto Jerusalem, and suffer many things of the elders and chief priests and scribes, and be killed, and be raised again the third day (Matthew 16:21).

Until this point, Jesus had not told His disciples anything about going to Jerusalem: the suffering, the crucifixion, or the resurrection. They were not ready to hear it. He knew that they would be ready in time, but there had to be certain truths established in their thinking before anything else of substance could be revealed to them. He could not teach them before they were ready. There is a time established by God for learning.

THE TIMING OF GOD

CHAPTER 4

An Appointed Time

There are certain truths that are going to have to be established in your heart and spirit as a foundation for God to build on. He cannot take you to second base until you have successfully reached first base. There are certain truths that have to be established in you before you are going to be able to go into the deeper things of God. Many times, we impede God's timetable because we have not done our homework. God wants to reveal things to us, but He cannot because we have not been as conscientious and diligent as we need to be with the things of God.

In verse twelve of Matthew twenty-six, Jesus said that the woman who put the oil on Him was anointing

Him for burial. This verse reads, "For in that she hath poured this ointment on my body, she did it for my burial" (Matthew 26:12). Jesus knew the ointment was for His burial. He was already in the sequence of events that would ultimately end His life. The gears had already been set in motion and could not be reversed by anyone other than Himself.

Jesus also had an appointed time to give Himself over to satan. Before that particular time, the devil could not touch Him; he tried, but failed. Satan hammered away at Him with everything he had. Among other things, he tried to have Him stoned. He tried everything imaginable to tempt Jesus and make Him fall, but he failed at every attempt—every single one.

> Now the first day of the feast of unleavened bread the disciples came to Jesus, saying unto him, Where wilt thou that we prepare for thee to eat the passover? And he said, Go into the city to such a man, and say unto him, The Master saith, My time is at hand; I will keep the passover at thy house with my disciples. And the disciples did as Jesus had appointed them; and they made ready the passover (Matthew 26:17-19).

The Father had an appointed time for Jesus to serve the Passover meal and go to Calvary. Jesus said, "My time is at hand." He would not try anything outside of God's timetable.

Moving Ahead of God

More Christians get in trouble by moving out ahead of the timing of God than probably anything else. It's not because their hearts are wrong, and it's not because they failed to hear from God. It's because they move too quickly for what God has planned. We have seen verse after verse, to establish that there is a time for everything.

Frustration comes to many Christians who attempt to start God-inspired, biblically legitimate ministries, but are failing in the process by circumventing God's timetable. They are stepping out in front of God's perfect timing and muscling their way through the process on their own. **Right thing; wrong time.**

Today is Always the Day of Salvation

Someone might ask, "What about the timing of salvation? Maybe my brother Sam isn't saved because it's not God's time to save him." Others may wonder about their husband or wife and thinking it may not be God's time to save them. The short answer is that you should be confident that salvation, healing, and even prosperity—anything that Jesus bought and paid for over two thousand years ago—has already been covered in His redemptive plan and is now yours for the asking. The Bible says that today is the day of salvation, and if you hear His voice, do not harden your heart. We do not need to wait on God's timing with regard to salvation because Jesus has already paid for it once and for all.

CHAPTER 5

Timing in God's Kingdom

Look at the fifth chapter of the Gospel of John. This is one of those truths, that when planted in your spirit and established in your thinking, will forever continue to bring a great deal of liberation and freedom into your life.

> Then answered Jesus and said unto them, Verily, verily, I say unto you, The Son can do nothing of himself, but what he seeth the Father do: for what things soever he doeth, these also doeth the Son likewise (John 5:19).

Being like Jesus, requires that we imitate Him by doing the things we see Him do and saying the things we hear Him say. Remember, Jesus never attempted anything outside of the timetable of God. He never attempted anything unless it was God's perfect time to do it.

Jesus said that He did not do anything in the earth except what He saw His Father do. Nothing else. We would be very prudent to follow His example and only do what we see our heavenly Father do.

Line Upon Line

There are timing considerations in God's Kingdom as well as our own personal lives. One event leads to another. One particular occurrence of something triggers a different and distinct result going forward. Additionally, your growth as a Christian is built, as the Bible says, line upon line, precept upon precept:

"For **precept** must be upon **precept, precept upon precept; line upon line, line upon line**; here a little, and there a little:" (Isaiah 28:10, emphasis added).

As an illustration, try to remember your time in high school algebra or other upper division math class. I think you would agree that it would be next to impossible to grasp the concepts of algebra, geometry, calculus, or trigonometry until basic math was mastered. Your Christian life works the same way. You cannot go directly to step two until step one is complete. There is not a substitute for going through the process because it prepares you for all the steps that follow.

CHAPTER 6

God's Blessing

We must all pay particular attention to the timing of God. Being a pastor, I must constantly be sensitive to His timing. Because I have always been open to listen to godly counsel concerning ministry ideas, I have had many people come to me with God-inspired, good, and worthy ideas and make suggestions concerning ministry projects. I must admit that I haven't implemented all of them, but I'm glad those people were comfortable enough to approach me. "Well, pastor," they would say, "I think we, as a church, should get involved in this particular ministry or take on that particular project."

At any one time, there are undoubtedly hundreds, if not thousands of viable projects that a church could possibly undertake, but they can't because the timing is not right.

THE TIMING OF GOD

Churches must remain obedient to their call, and the people in the churches must practice obedience. For instance, you might think a forty million dollar building is necessary to house and equip all the ministry God has called you to do. That may be a good idea, but I can assure you, you will only want to make that investment in God's timing. Even if you are one of those people who does not believe in timing and its importance, you need to know that Jesus certainly believed in it. That's why you can't do certain things; you are just not ready.

Jesus did not attempt to do anything except what He saw His Father do. Although I'm open for godly suggestions, I don't like to incorporate ministries into the church that have to be crutched up—constantly inspected on a daily basis—to make them work. If it can't stand on its own two feet, get rid of it.

On the other end of the spectrum, the one activity that I always see God bless is when I preach to our congregation in the sanctuary. When we congregate as a body to hear the Word of God and sing praises to the Lord, God always blesses it. Always. You need to pay attention to what God is blessing.

There are other things, however, that God really does not bless very much. For example, in most cases, it's not a really good idea to begin a ministry in your church just because—and for no other reason—than another church across town has been successful doing it. You need to hear God tell you to start it and not do it because some well-meaning person tickled your ear with the idea.

You would be surprised at the considerable numbers of people spending their time and money in numerous ministries that God has never asked them to do. God will probably bless their efforts to some level, but to a much larger degree, the obedient people will be rewarded for every single effort that they make. As they stand before God, they will be rewarded not only because of what was accomplished, but also because of their obedience to the call and the adherence to God's timing.

THE TIMING OF GOD

CHAPTER 7

God's Divine Timetable

> Then Jesus said unto them, My time is not yet come: but your time is alway ready. The world cannot hate you; but me it hateth, because I testify of it, that the works thereof are evil. Go ye up unto this feast: I go not up yet unto this feast: for my time is not yet full come (John 7:6-8).

Jesus told His disciples to go ahead without Him because it was not time for Him to go. Jesus never did things outside of the perfect timing of God.

I wish I had learned that truth a long time ago, but quite frankly, I have never heard much teaching on it; maybe some bits and pieces, here and there, but not much. The body of Christ desperately needs to hear it.

God has a divine timetable that must be followed. He has schedules and He has events. For example, there is an event scheduled in heaven called the marriage supper. It is an actual event on God's timetable. It is not starting today, and there is a good chance that it will not start tomorrow, but you can be confident that it will take place. Why? Because you and I have to be there! It is not starting without us. There is, without a doubt, a divine timetable.

Appointed Time of the Antichrist

Paul spoke to the Thessalonians about the Antichrist:

> "And now ye know what withholdeth that he might be revealed in his time" (2 Thessalonians 2:6).

Not surprisingly, there is even a specified time when the Antichrist is to be revealed. It is amusing to me, however, that many people have been caught up in various number games, attempting to determine who this person is. In fact, someone came up with a formula where a particular number was assigned to every letter of the alphabet, and after running these numbers concluded from this "mathematical formula" that a former Secretary of State is the Antichrist!

In the first place, it is not the time for the Antichrist to show up. You don't need to let the devil play mind games with you while you become a garbage dump for every deceiving spirit in town. Number games are not the same thing as receiving a revelation from God. Beware of letting your mind be manipulated. The Antichrist will be revealed in God's time.

By the way, just to end any speculation, we will already be in heaven when the Antichrist is finally revealed! We are going to be dancing up and down the streets of gold—swinging on the platinum chandeliers. When we're there, we are not going to be thinking about that guy, whomever he may be. I'm going to have my attention and my mind firmly focused on Jesus at the time.

The bottom line is the Antichrist can't be revealed except at God's appointed time in his divine timetable. There is a specific reason that he is not showing up right now, and that's because the church is still here.

THE TIMING OF GOD

CHAPTER 8

How to Miss the Will of God

I asked my wife, Nora, this question the other day and the way she answered it surprised me. I asked her, "Do you believe that it's possible for a faithful, dedicated, Bible-reading, praying, God-loving Christian to have a long-term desire in their heart that wasn't put there by God?"

She adamantly said, "Absolutely not! I don't believe that it's remotely possible." There's no room for interpretation in that answer. I don't believe it's possible either. I believe that after you have committed your heart to God and sold out to Him, most people miss His will by resisting it. Otherwise, we could be misled very badly. I'm not talking about flaky people who run around doing silly things; I'm talking about people who are sold out to God.

Christians should never struggle to find the will of God. As I said before, I truly believe **the only way to miss His will in your life is to resist it.** God will make it clear to you. At that point, the option is to obey or disobey, but He will get it over to you. You don't need to try all that hard; you just need to seek Jesus, and He'll tell you.

Creating a Desire

> For it is [not your strength, but it is] God who is effectively at work in you, both to will and to work [that is, strengthening, energizing, and creating in you the longing and the ability to fulfill your purpose] for His good pleasure (Philippians 2:13, AMP).

The Bible teaches that God is in you working, energizing, and creating the desire to do His will and pleasure in order to give you the desires of your heart. Psalm 37:4 says, "Delight yourself in the Lord, And He will give you the **desires** and petitions **of** your **heart** (AMP)." In other words, God will grant you the desires that are already in your heart, or He will actually place desires in there and then give them to you!

Some think that God will give His kids whatever they want. He will do that, especially when He puts those desires in there in the first place; however, it's a lot deeper than just giving you what you want. God is actually working in you telling you what you should want and then granting it to you.

It's good to know that those thoughts and desires that we receive from God and are still with us—those thoughts and desires that never seem to go away—are the will of God. We should immediately begin to set our lives in motion to pursue those desires. If you have had a strong desire for the last ten years to become a medical doctor, and the time has come to determine what track you are going to take in college, pursue medicine.

Distinguishing Your Call

You may say, "Well, maybe God's calling me to preach?" There is a big difference between being called into the ministry to preach and merely having a desire to preach because you love God and desire His Word. Unfortunately, Christians make that miscalculation all the time, and the devil leads them around by their noses. Be honest with yourself. Maybe you really don't want to be a preacher, but you erroneously think that God wants you to be one; you think that maybe He is going to be upset with you if you don't pursue that. You don't want to be on the "outs" with God so you keep that train of thought relentlessly moving on down the tracks of your mind. Do yourself a great favor, and stop thinking that way! You should never have to struggle to find God's will; He will make it clear to you.

In case you haven't figured it out yet, there could be a lying spirit talking to you about the ministry. Medical school is calling, and that is what you need to do. Here is some sagely advice for anyone in this position: do not go into the ministry unless you unquestionably know that you are called by God to do so. Whatever your call—be it the ministry, medicine, law, or business—do it, enjoy it, and work at it with all your might.

Avoid Distractions

People, for the most part, are sincere about their service to God and have a leading in their spirit that has been put there by Jesus. He may tell them some things that He wants them to do and possibly shown them glimpses of their future in the pursuit of His direction. Nevertheless, some distracting events are bound to happen.

For instance, someone may come up to you and prophesy that there is a worldwide ministry just waiting for you in your future. Although those words may be music to your ears, you need to be very careful and dodge that one in a hurry. You may have a dynamic worldwide ministry at some point, but you must wait on God if you're going to see it realized.

Leading of the Spirit

Here is a little more godly wisdom: if you go out today and try to make ministry happen on your own, you are going to be in serious trouble. You must wait on God's timing.

One of the quickest places to go hungry is in the ministry. People see successful ministers on television doing great things for God and think that they can do the same or better. They need to duck because they are getting ready to go broke very quickly and in a very big way. They may sincerely think that they can do it, but if they bypass Jesus Christ and His timetable, they can do nothing.

Trying to force yourself ahead of God's will and His timing, will only lead you into a frustrating existence with troubles all around and the possibility of tremendous personal lack and physical sickness. When you get out of the will of God, you are open to the devil and his maneuvers.

God, at times, through the leading of His spirit, will give us a glimpse of His plans for us. How else can we possibly know His will for us if He doesn't communicate it? Invariably, we get impatient and try to make it happen on our own by trying to perform things in the natural without waiting on God. It's important to know that **God does not need performers, He needs servants.** The church needs people who follow Jesus. Even when you have a pure heart and a glimpse of the future, the timing must still be right.

I heard someone say one of the most revealing statements that I have ever heard. He said, "If you want what God wants, for the reason that He wants it, and in the time that He wants it, there is nothing that you can't do. Nothing will be impossible for you." How profound. If you live by this, it will be a liberating truth to you and will take a great deal of friction out of your Christian life. We want to be able to live an abundant life without struggles, and that's what God wants for us, too.

THE TIMING OF GOD

CHAPTER 9

Time & Seasons

The book of Ecclesiastes talks about timing and purpose. In this book, King Solomon speaks about the seasons of our lives.

> "To every thing there is a season, and a
> time to every purpose under the heaven:"
> (Ecclesiastes 3:1).

This verse tells us that there is a season for everything. In many regions of the United States, we understand seasons and their variations. There is a transition from one season to another, and even without a calendar, we can feel it. We can tell when fall or summer arrives. We feel the change. There is a time, and there is a season.

Understanding Purpose

Let's talk about the word, *purpose*. There are things that God has purposed and planned for us, but there are times and seasons for those things. Noted pastor and teacher, the late Dr. Lester Sumrall, was the person most responsible for getting my mind on the right track concerning the issue of purpose and timing. He did it with a very short statement that the Holy Spirit drove into my heart.

I was in Houston Texas at a minister's conference many years ago. When Dr. Sumrall first came up to speak, he said, "There are some of you out there right now wondering why your ministries aren't doing any better than they are. It's simply because your time hasn't yet come." That's all he said. That's it. Then he went on to something else. It was truly a word that changed how I thought about things.

At that time, our ministry was doing well. Within two years of starting Redemption Church from nothing, we were seeing over three hundred people in our Sunday morning worship services. Today, we are accustomed to having many times more than that attend. Throughout our history, it has never been difficult getting people to listen and respond to the message of Jesus Christ. But, still, the truth that God has a timetable totally changed my thinking.

Changing Times

> To every thing there is a season, and a time to every purpose under the heaven: A time to be born, and a time to die; a time to plant, and a

> time to pluck up that which is planted; A time to kill, and a time to heal; a time to break down, and a time to build up; A time to weep, and a time to laugh; a time to mourn, and a time to dance; A time to cast away stones, and a time to gather stones together; a time to embrace, and a time to refrain from embracing; A time to get, and a time to lose; a time to keep, and a time to cast away. A time to rend, and a time to sew; a time to keep silence, and a time to speak; A time to love, and a time to hate; a time of war, and a time of peace. What profit hath he that worketh in that wherein he laboureth? I have seen the travail, which God hath given to the sons of men to be exercised in it. He hath made every thing beautiful in his time: also he hath set the world in their heart, so that no man can find out the work that God maketh from the beginning to the end (Ecclesiastes 3:1-11).

In Ecclesiastes, chapter three, the Bible speaks quite clearly concerning the different times and seasons that we encounter. There is a message here for all of us to contemplate. There are times when we are going to be doing a particular set of activities in our lives, and then there will be times when we're going to be putting those aside for more advanced endeavors. What we are doing today is not what we are going to be doing five years from now—or shouldn't be. We want to be growing and maturing consistently on a daily basis.

There is a time when we are going to have to hold on to what we have, but then there will be a time when God will tell us to let it go. Things change. We change. Times change. Don't get locked into one method. There's a time to do it one particular way, and then there's a time to change it up and do it another way.

There is a time when God deals with all of us. There is a time when He prunes us, shapes us, molds us, and ultimately perfects or matures us for His purpose.

CHAPTER 10

Willing & Obedient

I am extremely committed to Jesus. He is absolutely my best friend, and I do not have a great deal of desire or intention to please anyone in this entire world, except Him. If I can please others in the process of pleasing Him, so be it; but, if there comes a parting of the ways, I'm going with Jesus. I've expressed many times to the Lord that I will do whatever He wants me to do, even if I don't want to do it, because I want to please Him. But, I have also asked Him if He would allow me to actually have the desire to do that which He asks me to do! It's so much easier if you want to do it.

In Isaiah 1:19, God said that we would eat the good of the land if we are willing and obedient. There have been those times that I've approached God and told Him that I was in agreement with Him, but only by faith; I have told Him that I was "willing to be willing."

We all have struggles in our lives. You have them, and I have them as well. I know what you experience because I have experienced it, too. Even so, we must learn to respond to God in faith and be willing to obey Him.

Choose to be Willing

Some years ago, God told me to do something for Him which was altogether different from what I wanted to do. The decision I had to make was pulling at me relentlessly from two different directions—both sides could have been right and neither side would have been wrong. After days and days of struggling and agonizing over the decision, I finally got down on my face before God and humbly uttered these words to Him, "Whatever you want." At that time, I had to be willing to put my desires away and follow His plan.

Later on, I shared that experience with my wife, Nora, who had no idea of the struggle I was having. She immediately informed me that the Lord had recently given her a vision of an unknown man who was having a tremendous inner struggle and was torn between two opposing decisions. God knew the turmoil I was experiencing and had Nora praying for me! He knew one of His little boys was down here running around urgently needing to know what to do. This example shows us just how extremely important our problems and anxieties are to God. God's divine timetable will become clear to us, and we will have less obstacles as we are willing and obedient.

CHAPTER 11

He Cares for Us

I am committed to God, and He is, without question, committed to me. You would be crazy not to love someone who treats you that way. I am talking about God. I am talking about the Creator. I am talking about the Big Number One! There is none like Him. He is it. I am talking about the Biggest and the Best. I am talking about the Culmination of Everything.

Sometimes it's hard to think that God cares that much about me, but He does. Just me. Moreover, God cares about you the very same way. Just you. I know you've had a thought at one time or another that God would probably do something outstanding for someone else, but not for you. Let me assure you of something; if you are thinking that way, you are thinking incorrectly. He most certainly will do wonderful things for you, too! He sees the trouble you're in. He sees when life squeezes you. He sees the difficult time you are having. He cares so very much about the difficulties that you're experiencing and how uncomfortable life may have made you. He will put you on someone's heart before your next breath and have them praying for you. Think about it. I'm satisfied that there are people all over the world praying for me at my most challenging moments. I know they are, but I'll probably only know who they are when I get to heaven. I'll know it when the cork comes off the vial that's full of the prayers of the saints.

> And when he had taken the book, the four beasts and four and twenty elders fell down before the Lamb, having every one of them harps, and golden vials full of odours, which are the prayers of saints (Revelation 5:8).

It happens for you, too. It's not just for ministers; it's also for you. You are important to God. Your feelings and why you are feeling a particular way are important to God. Where you are spiritually, emotionally, and physically are important to Him, as well. He knows that your impatience, which is driven by your zeal for Him, makes you want to be somewhere else other than where you are. You want to be "in the game," not because you want to be out of His will, but because you want to get into His will. You have been there, haven't you? God knows exactly how you're feeling. Nevertheless, wait on Him. God has something beautiful for you, but you are going to have to give it the time it needs to make it work.

How do you determine how much time it will take before you see that beautiful thing that God has for you? I really can't tell you because it totally depends on what "beautiful" means to you. I don't know how much preparation it's going to take, but if God's going to do very much with you, it's going to take a little while to get you ready. Remember, Jesus ministered on this earth for three and one-half years, but it took thirty years to prepare Him.

THE TIMING OF GOD

CHAPTER 12

Let God Judge

"I said in mine heart, God shall judge the righteous and the wicked: for there is a time there for every purpose and for every work" (Ecclesiastes 3:17).

> Therefore judge nothing before the time, until the Lord come, who both will bring to light the hidden things of darkness, and will make manifest the counsels of the hearts: and then shall every man have praise of God (1 Corinthians 4:5).

Let me give you a good southern translation of these verses: don't judge what anyone else is doing. Don't attempt to judge something because you won't be able to see it accurately before you get to heaven—before the end of this life on earth. God is going to judge every man's works depending upon the purity and counsel of his heart. There will be some faithful intercessors that continually pray for ministers who have won countless thousands and maybe even millions of people to Jesus Christ; those intercessors may well receive greater rewards than the ministers themselves.

Don't judge anything before its time because much labor is done out of pure vanity. Popular evangelist James Robison talks about all the years he spent in activities he called "riding the horse" where he would try to manipulate the congregation's emotions in order to obtain positive results at the altar. He didn't know any other way to do it; he didn't know to let God work in hearts all by Himself. Just so you'll know, that kind of thing goes on all the time with other preachers as well, not just him.

But as you come clean with yourself and dig down into the recesses and the innermost workings of your heart, you will come to understand that it has to be God who orchestrates the outcomes in church and in life. You may just want to "ride the horse," "crutch it up," or muscle through on your own; however, there's a better way.

Allow God to Work

There are both denominational and full gospel preachers all over the world today who are mentally tormented to the point they can't stand it anymore; they've found themselves on a horse from which they can't get off. They are so financially committed—personally and for the ministry—they can't get out. They have found themselves so indebted to the process of ministry that they can't get away from it. Eventually, they get out of the ministry altogether because there is only so much a person can take. In one particular denomination, 2,700 ministers quit every year. You would quit too if you had to make the results happen on your own.

Ministers must learn that they have to allow God to interject Himself into every situation; we must walk and communicate with Him. This is not just a lesson for ministers; this is a word of truth for all of us. If God can't put you over, you don't need to be put over.

God Looks at the Heart

> "Humble yourselves therefore under the mighty hand of God, that he may exalt you in due time:" (1 Peter 5:6).

God bases His judgment on the heart—not on what we see taking place. The Bible says that we are to humble ourselves under the hand of God. We are to give Him preeminence by relinquishing control and giving Him the authority to run our lives. You might ask, "But why?" Because, when we humble ourselves under His hand, He may exalt us in due time. There is an exaltation that God has promised you, but it is in due time. "Due time" is His time.

The timing of the Lord is critical for everything God does. There is a place, a plan, and a purpose for you in the kingdom of God, and it calls for you to be exalted into everything He has promised you. There is a time for you to get off the bench and get in the game. There is a time for

THE TIMING OF GOD

your ministry and life to blossom, spring forth, and manifest, but it must be in His time.

God is the One who controls the timing. If we try to bypass His timing, the Bible says that we try to exalt ourselves and actually become abased. If you keep making the same mistake, you will keep going through the training process over and over again and never graduate.

CHAPTER 13

Focused on Him

God has a definite plan and purpose for you, but you are going to have to permit Him to work it out in your life. Some of you are called to do great and mighty exploits—marvelous, noble, and significant things for God. Some of you are called to lead many to righteousness while others are called to impact the gospel financially. God wants to promote some of you in the marketplace and channel enormous amounts of money into your hands so the gospel can be promoted around the world. God wants to make you a positive example in business in order to show others what great things a godly Christian businessperson can do by using the principles of sowing and reaping. God wants to put you there as long as your heart stays firmly focused on Him. He will not put anything into anyone's hands that could ultimately steal their heart away from Him.

God Will Prove You

Even though God does not test and try us with tribulations, He does prove His children. God will have us demonstrate to Him that we can be counted faithful. Our ability to receive, or not receive, depends on it. He also wants to see how we will respond to different events in different conditions.

If you find yourself in a difficult situation brought about by your failure to wait on God, He will certainly help you out of it; however, your relief might be longer in coming than you expected. Although He is a merciful God, He may let you live with your decision for a little while to see how you handle it. He is not an unkind, vindictive God; He merely wants to see if you pass the test. You know as well as I do that God can get you out of your predicament before morning; one snap of His heavenly fingers is all it takes. "So why do I keep staying in this mess?" you may ask. Maybe it is because you are not doing so well with the test. Don't keep taking the same test over and over again. Pass it, once and for all, and get promoted.

Remain Faithful

> And the things that thou hast heard of me among many witnesses, the same commit thou to faithful men, who shall be able to teach others also (2 Timothy 2:2).

The Bible says to commit the gospel to faithful men who have proven their faithfulness to God. God will not commit the gospel to a bunch of ungodly men and women. Do you think that He is going to let the oracles of God be proclaimed through someone who misleads people when their own lives are full of excess, wickedness, dishonesty, and all manner of sin? They may get by with their sin for a little while, but a day of reckoning will come; they will be exposed. The Bible teaches that we can be sure that our sins will find us out. When people act crazy doing inappropriate things and are unfaithful to God, unfaithful to the Word, and unfaithful to the things of God, they are not going to be trusted any longer—considering that He so graciously committed this glorious gospel to them in the first place.

Be Available

We carry around inside of us a holy gift; this is not something to be played with or to be looked at casually. It should not come as a surprise, but when you open up your Bible and begin reading, it is the God of the Universe speaking and revealing wonderful things to you. I am talking about God with a capital "G"! Why then do we tend to take it so casually? For instance, when you are experiencing financial problems, God will come to you and show you how to get out of them. He might even have a minister preach an entire message in order to help just one person in the congregation get out of the predicament in which they find themselves. Although many others will receive a great deal from the message, the Lord has that minister preach it just for one person sitting there in the twelfth row, third seat—you!

God does that for even a single one of His kids. He has had me do that exact thing. I have personally preached an entire message for one specific person, and the Holy Spirit has even revealed to me exactly who it was.

I do not preach *at* people from the pulpit; I preach truth *to* them. The truth from God's Word is what solves problems and sets people free. There is a sad truth, however. Many times when I preach, God has shown me by revelation knowledge that He wanted to set someone free, and that individual won't even be in the service. Their chance for a word from God at that moment is gone. He certainly may bring them a word for their problem again, but I am quite certain of this; even if they are not going to be serious with God's Word, He is still going to be serious with them.

You have probably witnessed the same thing. At one time, you may hear a message that you know in your heart is exactly what your Uncle Raymond needs to hear. He is sick and needs to hear that message on healing, but he decides to stay home and watch reruns of **The Andy Griffith Show**. God loves him enough to have the preacher bring a specific healing message to help him out of a bad situation, but he is not even there to receive his answer from God.

God will prove our hearts as we continue to serve Him. As we stay focused on Him, we must remain faithful and available to His leading and His delivering hand.

CHAPTER 14

A Time to Mature

Many of us have asked the question, "When is God going to exalt me?"

> "And let us not be weary in well doing: for
> in due season we shall reap, if we faint not"
> (Galatians 6:9).

There is a time for reaping and there is a time for sowing. Please notice, however, the people who reap are the ones who do not faint. It is not automatic that you are going to reap regardless of what you do. It is, however, automatic that you will reap if you obey God, follow His Word, and do not faint.

Remain Under Authority

> Now I say, That the heir, as long as he is a child, differeth nothing from a servant, though he be lord of all; But is under tutors and governors until the time appointed of the father (Galatians 4:1-2).

These verses are talking about you being an heir of God and a joint heir with Christ Jesus. This truth comes straight out of Galatians chapters three and four which talks about you being an heir of God and an heir of the blessings of Abraham. If you are in Christ, then you are Abraham's seed and heirs according to the promise. It then takes you directly into chapter four. Let's look at these verses together:

> There is neither Jew nor Greek, there is neither bond nor free, there is neither male nor female: for ye are all one in Christ Jesus. And if ye be Christ's, then are ye Abraham's seed, and heirs according to the promise. Now I say, That the heir, as long as he is a child, differeth nothing from a servant, though he be lord of all; But is under tutors and governors until the time appointed of the father (Galatians 3:28-4:2).

Each of us, as believers, have access to the entire universe and every blessing that God will ever give. However, if we do not mature and grow up, we are never going to come out from under the tutors and governors set over us. Even if we are maturing and growing up, there is still a need to spend time under authority. To arrive at God's appointed time, you must take time to develop. God has an appointment with you, and on that day, He will tell you to step out into the work that you have been called. **Commit to stay under your tutors and governors until God calls you out; do not step out just because you think you are ready.**

Stay Committed

One reason why God does not like people constantly moving around from church to church is because it shows a lack of commitment. Have you ever noticed the people who constantly change churches are never there when you need them? They are never faithful, never committed, and never there when it's time to work. They always seem to be off on some spiritual journey or at some Christian concert. Conversely, **the journey you're on depends a great deal on diligence and hard work.** Stay committed and stay with something until you see it produce, and let God deal with your life and develop you in the process.

Learn from Your Mistakes

God has to properly train His children before they can come forth. He can't trust you with a million dollars until you're faithful with a hundred. If you are given a hundred dollars and blow it all on lottery tickets, God is not going to give you a big suitcase full of money. There has to come a time when you develop yourself and work with what you have been given; there's a point where you come to the point that you can handle what God wants you to have. That's the Lord proving us, not testing and trying us.

THE TIMING OF GOD

For instance, if you've been struggling with the same financial difficulties for the last forty-five years, it seems to me that you would have had plenty of time to learn how to fix the problem and learn how to handle money. If you have never passed the money test, you probably need to stay under your tutors until you learn it. If you have been at it for forty-five years and it hasn't worked, you are going to have to change the way you are going about the problem-solving process.

You would be amazed at how many people keep doing the same things that are binding them week in and week out, month in and month out, year in and year out. It bound them last year, and it is binding them again this year, but they keep doing the same things over and over again expecting a different result. That's the definition of *insanity*. You may quickly offer the excuse that what you're doing is believing God to help you. This is not how you believe God; you have to change, and sometimes change can be hard.

CHAPTER 15

Promoting the Kingdom

> "Jesus saith unto them, My meat is to do
> the will of him that sent me, and to finish
> his work" (John 4:34).

Jesus said that His only satisfaction was to do the will of His Father. Likewise, our only desire should be to do the will of God or to do what we see Him do. Our pursuits in ministry must never be to promote ourselves. Unfortunately, a great deal of efforts in ministry are done for self-promotion.

A few years ago during our earlier years in ministry, we contacted a Christian singer—a tremendous man of God who really loves the Lord—to hold a concert in our church.

THE TIMING OF GOD

It would have been a great blessing to us and to the city. We had a problem with the invitation, however, when we found out it was going to cost us thousands of dollars for a two-hour concert. This singer was so encumbered with financial obligations that he could not afford to come at a more reasonable rate.

There are ministers who find themselves in that same situation. They have so many financial commitments that they cannot afford to go to smaller churches. Is that wrong? Not exclusively, but it is wrong if God tells you to go to a smaller church, and you are unable due to your financial issues. It's not necessarily wrong to have obligations as you go about promoting the gospel, but if God tells you minister at a little church, you'd better pack your bag and get over there in a hurry! Not all ministry is of God. A lot of it is just shouldering responsibilities and doing things out of sheer grit—promoting self and not Jesus. This is how we—ministers and laymen—get ourselves into bondage.

Someone might say, "I have to be a star!" No, you don't. Jesus is the star. You don't have to be anything. You just have to follow the Lord. It's much sweeter that way. Isn't it funny that no one is ever called to smaller churches?

I don't know about you, but I want to enjoy this trip through life. God will exalt you in due time, so let Him develop you, train you, and bring you into your own. Less sweat and more sweet; that's how I like it.

If It's Not of God, Let It Go

Reverend James Robison once shared how he had struggled with the very things that we've been talking about. He shared that he had two million dollars in overdue television bills and other obligations. So what did he do? He went to the Bible, got before God, and said, "Listen, God, if this ministry's not of you, then just let it die. I don't even care."

Jesus told him that the answer to his dilemma was that he was going to have to minister to the entire body of Christ, not just the Baptist Church. He went immediately to his staff and told them what he was going to do. But, instead of seeing enthusiasm in them, his staff started to dwindle away from over 150 people to only fifty; that's a sixty-six percent drop in staff. Instead of getting better, his problems seemed to multiply. However, because he was obedient and didn't get ahead of God's timing, he went from being two million dollars behind in his bills to thirty days ahead! It's nothing but a struggle to make something work totally on your own and without having help from heaven in your corner.

It is not just the James Robisons of the world either; it is every one of you, too. Is there something that you feel like you have to do for God, but instead you're out trying to make it work on your own? It's time to stop and let God make it work. Give Him freedom in your life. God will make it work subject to His holy timetable. Don't shoulder all the responsibility for the success of that thing on your own. Let God take care of things in His way and in His time.

Don't Forget Your Call

There have been times in your life, I'm sure, when God has dealt with your heart to do something for Him that you thought seemed a little below your call. I caution you, however, to remember that God said to take heed to the ministry that you've been given in order that you fulfill it.

There was a time in my life when I was struggling. I was going before God needing answers because I wanted to do something else. I told God that I had to hear from Him; I had to hear His voice because I needed an answer.

I don't know any better way to hear the voice of God than to go to the Bible. As I opened my Bible, God took me straight to Colossians 4:17 which reads, "And say to Archippus, Take heed to the ministry which thou hast received in the Lord, that thou fulfil it."

I read it, and God spoke again saying, "You'd better take heed and do what I told you to do, sonny boy. I told you to do something, and I didn't tell you to get it half done either. You can go and do what you want to do, but I'm going to tell you right now that if you do, you're walking out on me." It didn't take me long to make my decision! I planted my feet firmly in the ground and did not move from doing what God told me to do. You have probably been there in some fashion, as well.

Complete the Work

Have you ever felt the need to go do something, but you're not sure just what you're going to do? **If you don't have direction or something concrete from God, complete the last thing He told you to do before you start anything else.** Just finish what you know to do and accomplish the task God gave you because then you'll be a prime candidate for a promotion.

Conversely, if you decide to go out on your own, ahead of God's timing, you will be a prime candidate for a huge failure. You will have to stay in school until you learn the lessons that you failed to learn the first time through. There are preachers who have been in ministry for forty years who have never learned that truth.

THE TIMING OF GOD

CHAPTER 16

A Time to Prepare

The apostle Paul spoke about preparation in his letter to the Ephesians:

> "And your feet shod with the preparation of the gospel of peace" (Ephesians 6:15).

Ephesians says your feet are shod with the "preparation" of the gospel. If you are not prepared, you are not "properly shod"—you are not wearing the proper footwear to complete your task effectively. In fact, it is akin to being barefooted. Ladies, if you are going to spend the day hiking in the mountains, would you wear a pair of high heels or go barefooted? In the same way, you men would probably not choose hockey skates to finish off that tuxedo you're wearing to the opera with your wife. You would be improperly shod and look silly in the process. If you are wearing the right shoes or are "properly shod," you are prepared for whatever lies ahead. The way to become properly shod in the spirit is to take time to let God establish and prepare your ministry.

Jesus Waited for His Time

God has established a timetable for each of us. He wants us to be in agreement with His timing and not barreling ahead with our own. It is hard for us, as believers, to just sit and wait, but we must. We cannot grab at something just because it looks enticing. Not everything that comes along is good; not everything that comes along is God.

> These words spake Jesus, and lifted up his eyes to heaven, and said, Father, the hour is come; glorify thy Son, that thy Son also may glorify thee: (John 17:1).

Jesus was the greatest example of someone who was totally committed to following God and going along with His Father's timetable. We must also be committed to following God's timetable concerning our lives and ministries.

Jesus was very aware that there were specific times for particular events to take place. He said, "My hour is come." He knew it in His spirit. He did not try to force Himself to the cross early. He didn't try to force the things that were already destined and predestined to happen to Him. He did not try to force things to happen before their appointed time. There was a specific time for Him, just like there is a specific time for us.

Maturing in Your Call

Many times, we faith people confess our way into things that we eventually wish we hadn't. Why? Because the timing is not right; it's too soon. We're not mature enough to handle it.

As parents, for example, we are totally convinced that our children are unable to respond beyond their level of maturity. For example, you would never allow your five-year-old daughter to hop in the driver's seat of your car and drive it down the street because it would be incredibly irresponsible. There has to be time for development. There certainly will be a time that she will be able to drive that car, but the state says she cannot legally drive by herself until she is sixteen years old and holds a valid driver's license. However, we both know that just because they are of legal age doesn't mean they possess the maturity and the responsible attitude that driving requires. Some young people do, but some don't. You, as parents, need to take on the responsibility to make that call. In the same way, God is the one who makes that call with regard to our maturity and our destiny.

Responsible Riches

Did you know that God has promised riches to His children? The Bible says that Jesus was made poor so that you could be made rich.

> For ye know the grace of our Lord Jesus Christ, that, though he was rich, yet for your sakes he became poor, that ye through his poverty might be rich (2 Corinthians 8:9).

This verse simply means wealth. However, many times, when it comes to money, God cannot give believers what He has promised in His Word because they are too irresponsible. They have not learned and developed the skills needed to handle money. God wants to give His kids the riches He promised, but He can't. It is not yet their time because they have not learned the money lesson yet. They have to go back to school. They still need their tutors when they should actually be teaching the class. Make a decision that you won't miss your appointed time.

We Are Heirs

> And if ye be Christ's, then are ye Abraham's seed, and heirs according to the promise. Now I say, That the heir, as long as he is a child, differeth nothing from a servant, though he be lord of all but is under tutors and governors until the time appointed of the father (Galatians 3:29-4:2).

We saw earlier in these verses that all of us who are in Christ are His heirs; we are joint heirs with Jesus Christ. If you are Christ's, then you are Abraham's seed and heirs according to the promise.

As long as the heir is still a child and is spiritually immature, he is viewed in the same way as a servant, even though he is the master of everything. God has made His heirs "lord" of the universe. Being a joint heir with Christ Jesus is the conduit that gives us that privilege. Jesus is Lord, and we are seated together with Him in the heavenlies. Our heavenly

Father gave us "lordship" when we received Christ and were born again, but as long as we remain spiritually immature, we are no different than a servant. We have to go back to school.

The Bible calls for an appointed time to make transitions. There is first a preparation phase when we prepare ourselves to be faithful in the essential areas of our life and ministry. Later, as we show ourselves faithful and become more proficient in our areas of responsibility, we will begin to emerge and be entrusted with more of God's ministry and resources. Yet, if we come to the appointed time to step out, and we are not found to be responsible with the things of God, our prearranged time will come and go, and we will remain servants even though in God's eyes we are "lord" of all.

THE TIMING OF GOD

CHAPTER 17

A Time for Action

Think back to the book of Matthew when Jesus said that His time was at hand. He said there was a definitive time in God's timetable for His purpose to be manifested.

> "And he said, Go into the city to such a man, and say unto him, The Master saith, My time is at hand;" (Matthew 26:18).

If you will also recall from the book of John when Jesus said that He only did the things He saw His Father do.

> Then answered Jesus and said unto them, Verily, verily, I say unto you, The Son can do nothing of himself, but what he seeth the Father do: for what things soever he doeth, these also doeth the Son likewise (John 5:19).

Jesus didn't walk ahead of God. He waited on His Father's perfect timing. Everything was built line upon line, precept upon precept.

Proceed with Caution

As a church or a ministry, we have to be cautious not to overextend ourselves. We can provide so many ministries and services within the church that it becomes overwhelming. In the area of finances, a church in its beginning stage cannot do as much ministry as an established fifty year-old church can. The older, established church has a stronger footing and a stronger financial base.

At the beginning stages of any ministry, it's easy to become overextended. We must therefore be cautious in everything we do because if our zeal outweighs our knowledge, we can overextend many of our resources. We have to be cautious not to get ourselves in trouble financially. In a ministry, it's also easy to overextend our time and our human resources. Overextending can happen to us in our personal lives as well as in the ministry.

As a pastor, there are certain things that I have to be cautious of while providing leadership to a congregation. Looking back to our very early years, and remembering some of the decisions we made, it is a wonder that we still exist! Much of the time, our zeal overpowers our knowledge. We had to diligently go through the process of learning what we needed to do that we were not already doing; what we needed to do better; and, just as importantly, what we needed to eliminate and never do again! It's the process of the local body growing and developing.

With that said, my advice is: get your feet wet and go. Pray a lot, and get on with it. If you keep your heart right with God, He will correct many of the problems that will surely arise.

Although God is full of grace and mercy regarding your personal mistakes, never become cavalier concerning Scripture. If we remember this, we can be aggressive and know that God will help us in our learning process. As we learn, we become more capable in the process of dealing with various situations. Also in that learning process, there will be many mistakes and many victories. So, we pray a lot to cover the mistakes that we are sure to make. In doing this, we become sharper and keener; we mature and we grow.

No Time for Shortcuts

"Yea, so have I strived to preach the gospel, not where Christ was named, lest I should build upon another man's foundation" (Romans 15:20).

Paul said that he would not build on another man's foundation. There are no shortcuts. Many things have to be done, line upon line, precept upon precept if we want our foundation to be firmly established.

Did that mean that Paul failed to recognize anyone else's work in the Lord? Not at all. He was saying that he could not afford to establish his spirituality based solely on some other person's relationship with God. We can't either. We must experience Jesus and experience the heavenly Father for ourselves and learn about the Holy Spirit on our own.

THE TIMING OF GOD

CHAPTER 18

Responsible Living

"Surely goodness and mercy shall follow me all the days of my life: and I will dwell in the house of the Lord for ever" (Psalm 23:6).

The Psalmist says that when the Lord is guiding us as the Great Shepherd, we can be certain that goodness and mercy will follow us all the days of our lives. What a great promise! When we are convinced that we've just made the world's most terrible mistake, and there is no way out, God says that He'll come in with a big boatload of mercy and fix it up. Be careful, though, because that **mercy doesn't allow us to be purposefully negligent in our duties.** We can't be slothful in the things of God, yet when the need arises we can throw ourselves and our ignorance over on His mercy.

Put Away Childish Things

Let me reiterate this truth: there is "a time" in the Kingdom. In the Bible, the apostle Paul said:

> When I was a child, I spake as a child, I understood as a child, I thought as a child: but when I became a man, I put away childish things (1 Corinthians 13:11).

There is a time for playing with toys, and there is a time to put them away. Do you remember several years ago during the Christmas season, when countless adults wanted desperately to purchase Cabbage Patch dolls? They were literally fighting each other in order to get their hands on them. These silly little dolls were in relatively short supply, and grown men and women were acting like spoiled children trying to buy them. Adults fighting over dolls! Who would have thought? People were obsessed with them. Some thought they were going to make a lot of money with those dolls when the supply dwindled, and some just wanted to collect them. It wasn't the dolls or the collectors that I took issue with, but the supremely childish act of fighting over them. Although there are many things adults do that are childlike, there is a time to put away those childish things.

The Proper Season

The book of Ecclesiastes is quite adamant on the subject of "times and seasons."

> To every thing there is a season, and a time to every purpose under the heaven: A time to be born, and a time to die; a time to plant, and a time to pluck up that which is planted; (Ecclesiastes 3:1-2).

There is a time when God says to come out of where you are and move on up to a higher place. There is a time when leaves fall off the trees, and there is a time when they grow back again. There are times and seasons that you simply cannot change. You can stand out in your yard under a huge oak tree all spring and command the leaves to fall off, but the leaves are going to stay right where they are. It is just not the right season. Go yell at those same leaves in the fall, and you might get some satisfaction, but not in the spring. The point is: **you cannot confess your way into the blessings of God until the proper season**.

You may be confessing prosperity Scriptures every day, but you must remember that you have to go through a process of development before you are able to receive what God has for you. The process of learning and developing causes many people to be greatly frustrated in their everyday faith life. We most certainly can have the blessings and the prosperity of God, but there is a season for it in our lives. God will make everything beautiful in His time, but He has to develop and train us so we'll be ready.

God has to teach us how to be responsible so the blessings won't be damaging to our relationship with Him. All of us have to go through that process, but some of us are a bit more pliable and learn more quickly than others. Some people may choose to be bull-headed and stubborn which draws out the process.

There are those of us who were fortunate enough to have grown up in a godly home with parents who taught us the Word of God. However, if you are not in that category and didn't receive a godly foundation at a young age, it is still your responsibility to make the effort to learn these things.

God's Stewards

One of the reasons many entertainers turn away from God is because of the enormous wealth that is suddenly dumped in their laps. Many of them have no clue how to manage money at that level; they haven't had the proper training they need to make good decisions with their money and just go wild with it. They are totally irresponsible. Conversely, an individual from a wealthy family—trained in the proper way to handle money since childhood—can handle larger amounts of money. They handle money more effectively than the person who has received sudden wealth with no training at all.

We experience that same thing in the world of the spirit and in our relationship with the Lord. God said if you haven't been faithful in material things, He won't trust you with true spiritual riches.

> "If therefore ye have not been faithful in the unrighteous mammon, who will commit to your trust the true riches?" (Luke 16:11).

Responsible Living

There is a principle involved here that says **we are stewards of God's resources, and we must show ourselves worthy of the things that God has given us.**

THE TIMING OF GOD

CHAPTER 19

God Will Develop You

As Christians, we have to grow and wait on the timing of the Lord. Remember when you were six years old and how much you wanted to be seven? You couldn't get there fast enough. When you were thirteen, you wanted to be sixteen so you could drive a car. When you were sixteen, you wanted to be twenty-one so you could vote...among other things.

When we go through this process of development, we must be mindful to prevent a seed of dissatisfaction from taking root in our lives. I believe that a lot of dissatisfaction is from the devil, trying to cause us to be discontented with our position in life. People always want to be somewhere other than where they are. You may recognize the well-used idiom, "The grass is always greener on the other side of the fence."

But, believe me when I say it's not. From a far distance, a pasture can look like a velvet carpet, but when you get closer and step over in it, you realize that the grass is halfway to your knees, and the ground is lumpy and uneven—nothing pristine about it. Things are not always as they seem.

The devil plants these seeds of dissatisfaction to keep us from being faithful where we are. He plants the desire that makes us always want to change and move on, never establishing roots. *Be careful not to confuse this impulsive leading that tends to send us in every direction imaginable, with a God-inspired holy dissatisfaction that's used to help lead us in God's direction.* I'm not saying that we shouldn't be stirred to activity, but that activity should be God-motivated, stable, and focused in a particular direction. It should be centered on God's Word and not just activity for the sake of activity. **Zeal without knowledge produces nothing except a lot of frustration and trouble.**

One Day at a Time

> "I said in mine heart, God shall judge the righteous and the wicked: for there is a time there for every purpose and for every work" (Ecclesiastes 3:17).

There is a time for every purpose and for every work, and we have to allow that timing to work in our lives. We can't force God's perfect timing to come about.

Experience, for us, comes one day at a time. Someone once said to me that experience is not the best teacher; the Word of God is the best teacher. True enough, but experience is a good teacher as well.

If you went out to an airport and hopped on a Boeing 747 for a flight to Hong Kong, you would want a seasoned, trained, experienced, textbook pilot behind the stick of that airplane. You would want someone in the pilot's seat who had flown that gigantic aircraft many times before. You would want a pilot who had gone to flight school and studied all the required material—learned about the altimeter and attitude indicators and was more than familiar with the function of the ailerons, flaps, elevator, and rudder. You would want him to know what switches to flip and what buttons to push, and just as importantly, when to do it. Pilots know better than most people about the proper timing of taking on that next level of responsibility; they know what it takes before they actually sit down in that captain's chair. They learn all the procedures before they ever take that plane off the ground—even before they solo the very first time. Before they go up and fly that airplane, they have to absorb a massive amount of information from the books. However, they are still not pilots until they actually fly that plane.

It's the same way with biblical matters. Preparation and experience from the Word of God can keep us from crashing our spiritual airplane, just like proper preparation and experience keeps the pilot from crashing the plane for which he's been properly trained. If all we know is what we saw in the Bible and never experience it in our daily lives, we have not become trustworthy, reliable soldiers of Jesus Christ. **Use the Word to live with and to live by.** Experience just simply comes one day at a time. You cannot make it come more quickly, and you can't slow it down.

A Time to be Promoted

> "Humble yourselves therefore under the mighty hand of God, that he may exalt you in due time:" (1 Peter 5:6).

God intends to exalt you in due time and in His season. There is a due time and a due season when God will begin to promote you. The Bible says in the book of Psalms that promotion doesn't come from the east, west, or south; it comes from above. In this verse, we learn that God elevates one and puts down another.

> For promotion cometh neither from the east, nor from the west, nor from the south. But God is the judge: he putteth down one, and setteth up another (Psalm 75:6-7).

When we show ourselves faithful to God, walk with Him, spend time with Him, and allow the timing of the Lord to work in our lives, it's then that we are ready to move on. But when we try to force the timing of God, we are going to find ourselves being moved back to square one again. We are going to have to go back to school because God said if you try to exalt yourself, you will be abased or pushed down. It's like depressing a button. God wants to exalt you, but He wants it to happen in His time. Doing it His way will ensure that you can handle the promotion, and it won't damage you or hurt other people.

A Time for Establishing

Many times, the reason that it takes so long for ministries to become established is that the individuals involved must first prove themselves faithful. We have all heard of ministers who were promoted in the Kingdom, and the ear of the Christian world listened to them. This gave them a great following, but they ultimately failed. It hurt those ministers to fail, but you also have to think about all the other people who were damaged in the process. That's why I endeavor as a pastor and as a minister to be responsible before God concerning the people and the work. I care too much about the people of God to slip-up. I don't want your life to fail before God, so I have to be mature and responsible.

I remember back when I first started seriously studying the Word of God; it was one day up and two days down. You remember those days, don't you? Some of you reading this book are still going through them. I'm now to a place in God where I'm not up and down anymore. There are times, however, I find my activities and my schedule restrict my time with Him, but I never have days that I just lose it and choose to go sin. I no longer do that, but it's a process of development. Today, my low days are better than my high days used to be.

Your life is that way, too. Look back at where you were several years ago and where you are now. God is developing you and bringing you to a place where you can be more responsible and receive more from Him. Then, the blessings can come your way and not damage you or hurt you and the people around you.

We have to let God develop us. Even when we get to heaven, the growth process will go on—it will go on throughout eternity. God said that He will show us exceeding grace through all the ages to come.

Time in Eternity

When you get to heaven, you are going to be looking forward to coming back to earth with King Jesus. It's like being away from somewhere you really loved for a long period of time, and you want to go back just to see it—like revisiting your childhood home. When we are in heaven at the marriage supper of the Lamb, and we are awaiting Jesus' return to Earth, the Bible says that we shall (future tense) rule and reign with Him. He's still speaking of the future even after we are already in heaven. You may have thought that time ceased there, but evidently not. The question remains to be answered: how can there be a future if time ceases?

The King James Version of the Bible says that time shall be no more, but just not how we're thinking about it. Another translation states:

> And he swore by him who lives for ever and ever, who created the heavens and all that is in them, the earth and all that is in it, and the sea and all that is in it, and said, "There will be no more delay!" (Revelation 10:6, NIV).

Time is going to go on forever. However, the issues that time brings will be a thing of the past; there will be no more death and decay.

There still will be a future when you go to heaven. How can there be an age to come if there is no future? You are going to continue to grow throughout the ages to come. The more responsible you are here, the more responsible you will be there. This growth process will perpetuate itself forever. So, we must show ourselves faithful to God in this lifetime.

THE TIMING OF GOD

CHAPTER 20

Faithful to Your Call

> And the things that thou hast heard of me among many witnesses, the same commit thou to faithful men, who shall be able to teach others also (2 Timothy 2:2).

The prerequisite to be able to teach others is faithfulness. Teaching is not just standing up, reading the Word of God and teaching a passage of Scripture. Teaching is more than that.

Bible teaching includes in it the ability to express the nature and the character of God. Paul says to follow him as he follows God. He does not say to follow only the things he says, but to follow his example. The highest authority you have is God, and you should never follow anyone who doesn't follow Him. Nevertheless, if a person is following God, you absolutely need to pattern your life after them—trying to express the attributes and qualities that God is expressing through them. For example, if someone knows how to pray, then you should follow their example when you pray. Follow them as they follow God.

Proper Motives

There were times in my life when I really wanted people to know that I was there and that I mattered. I felt the same way that the professional football player feels who wants everyone to recognize his athletic ability, or the young entrepreneur who thinks he's the next Steve Jobs, or the twelfth ranked heavyweight boxer who believes he's every bit as good as Muhammad Ali was in his prime.

I really just wanted people to hear the Word of God. That, in and of itself, wasn't wrong; however, the way I wanted to go about it needed some work. I wanted people to hear God's Word, and I wanted to use a huge convention of twenty thousand people to deliver it. At the time, I thought the only reason I wanted to be there was so people would hear the Word, but down inside there was probably a lot of "self" involved. The reason might have been that I just wanted someone to know I was there; however, I don't think I recognized that at the time. I genuinely don't think that my heart was wrong, but I realize now that the way I wanted to do it was.

Along life's way, I think all of us experience many things that we don't recognize or understand due to our immaturity at the time. When you're in that position, you may find that you begin to maneuver yourself to try and make big things happen on your own. That's the time to be careful. You're really getting ready to slip up. God wants you there, and He knows how to get you there. I believe with all my heart that I'll be there; but, there is a time, and I'll know when that time arrives. I also know that I have to play by the rules, and I have to stay close to the Spirit of God. You have to take heed to the ministry that God has given you and make sure you accomplish what God wants you to do.

God's Plan in My Life

Many years ago now, God told me to come to Knoxville, Tennessee and establish a church. I am so convinced of it that if an angel were to fly in the room, buzz around, stand right in front of me, and tell me that I was wrong, I would tell that angel, "You don't know whereof you speak, Mr. Angel. I am totally convinced."

A little while later, I felt like God was speaking to me about traveling around the world. That's a really exciting proposition. It would have been very easy to start thinking too much about the travel and not enough about establishing the church. I could have also tried to strong-arm it to make it happen on my own. At the time, however, it was mere speculation. So I wisely decided to follow God's plan and His timing for my life. I stayed the course for establishing the church and waited on God's timing. I know now that He put world travel in my heart to keep me running toward a goal. I can truthfully say after visiting most every continent on the earth and traveling to well over sixty nations—some of them multiple times—that you can't argue with God's timing.

Long-range goals are vital, but don't let them cause you to neglect what God wants you to do right now. Take heed to the ministry that God has called you into; don't leave it early and see that you fulfill it. If you leave it before you accomplish what God told you to accomplish, you have been unfaithful to Him. The gospel is committed to the faithful, and if you leave early, you have shown yourself unfaithful in a commission that He entrusted to you.

Moreover, if God tells you to go out on a gravel road and preach to the rocks, you had better go preach to them. I know you want to go preach to all the excited, God-loving people who clap, jump, and cheer; but, there are a bunch of rock-hard knuckleheads who need to be preached to as well. Interestingly enough, very few people like to go preach to them.

Step by Step

During that time when I was young in the ministry, I was under the naïve impression that just because we were in the will of God and were being obedient to Him, we were going to come back to Knoxville, do what God told us to do, and automatically have ten thousand people show up at our Sunday morning services. Everything was going to be great. Sometimes, I'm sure you know, reality is a hard taskmaster.

Believe it or not, I'm really thankful that it didn't happen that way. I think about all the unsuspecting members of our church who would have been negatively affected if it had. A pastor needs to learn how to pastor a church—beginning with smaller congregations and then working up. You don't just walk in one day having no experience and automatically know how to run a church—small or large. You have to learn how. Over a period of years, God has taught me some supremely important pastoring lessons. I certainly don't know everything, but I know substantially more than I once did.

God is Big Enough

As I mentioned earlier, I believe the only way that you can miss the will of God is to actually resist it. I believe that God has the ability to tell you what He wants you to do in a way that you'll understand. I also believe that after He tells you, there is a choice that you have to make to either act on it or dismiss it.

We need to spend time with the Lord and separate ourselves from the noises of everyday life to hear His voice more effectively. We should not have to struggle in a cluttered world to hear God as He speaks to us. Get away from the noise and unclutter yourself. He knows where you live, and He is certainly capable of telling you what He wants you to do. In the event He doesn't tell you anything, simply continue what you're doing.

THE TIMING OF GOD

CHAPTER 21

Persevere to the End

> "And say to Archippus, Take heed to the ministry which thou hast received in the Lord, that thou fulfil it" (Colossians 4:17).

The gospel is committed to faithful men. The Bible says that we are to take heed to the ministry that we've been given and to fulfill it. Don't stop short. Don't quit.

Walking in the will of God is never easy. Once you have heard the voice of the Lord and said "yes" to Him, walking in the will of God and getting yourself into the perfect center of His will could possibly be the hardest battle you will ever fight.

Staying in the will of God will be the hardest struggle you will ever face. Why? Because there will always be little carrots of opportunities dangled in front of you, designed to draw your attention away from your primary purpose. One person will tell you to do something that sounds exciting, and another will tell you about something else that seems even better. I am not saying that you should turn down every opportunity, but if those opportunities take you away from the ministry for which Jesus has made you accountable, you'd better avoid them. Don't give them a place in your thought process. God not only told you to find His will and begin, He told you to complete the work. Starting isn't enough; you must finish.

Jesus Finished the Work

> "I have glorified thee on the earth: I have finished
> the work which thou gavest me to do"
> (John 17:4).

How did Jesus glorify His Father? He finished the work that His Father gave Him to do. This is what caused such a struggle for Jesus in the Garden of Gethsemane.

> Saying, Father, if thou be willing, remove this cup from me: nevertheless not my will, but thine, be done. And there appeared an angel unto him from heaven, strengthening him. And being in an agony he prayed more earnestly: and his sweat was as it were great drops of blood falling down to the ground (Luke 22:42-44).

At the beginning, Jesus didn't know if He was going to go through with the process that led up to His crucifixion. Why do you think He was sweating blood? He asked His Father if there was any other way to accomplish God's purpose because He didn't want to do it. I am forever grateful that Jesus went through with it. Humanity would be in great trouble right now if He had not completed His work.

Jesus knew the will of God and went through with the plan to its fruition. Finishing it, I can promise you, wasn't easy. Conversely, many people absolutely know God's will for themselves, but never finish what God asked them to do. They start out strong, but some unforeseen incident or circumstance hinders their progress, and the importance of the plan fades away. They hear the voice of the Lord, agree to the commission He offers, but decide, for whatever reason, that it isn't worth the effort. They simply walk away and think everything is wonderful.

Determine to Finish

It is one thing to be on the perimeter of the will of God when you are a new Christian, but it's another thing altogether to enter into the very center of His will. We have all asked God to allow us to enter into His perfect will at one time or another. Did He then point out to you what He told Ananias to tell Paul?

> "For **I will shew him how great things he must suffer** for my name's sake" (Acts 9:16).

God did not tell Ananias to let Paul know what a cozy and warm bed of luxurious comfort he was getting himself into. No, He said to go down there and tell Paul all the things he must suffer for the gospel. Paul had the choice right then to decline the offer and would have still gone to heaven and danced up and down the streets of gold. We would still meet him when we get to heaven, but he wouldn't mean as much to us because he would not have written half the New Testament. When Paul decided to go God's way and determined that he would get in the perfect center of the will of God, demon forces tried to stop him at every turn, but Paul didn't quit.

> But none of these things move me, neither count I my life dear unto myself, so that I might finish my course with joy, and the ministry, which I have received of the Lord Jesus, to testify the gospel of the grace of God (Acts 20:24).

Paul said the things he experienced did not dissuade him. What did a few shipwrecks, stonings, and beatings have to do with anything? No big deal. Those things did not move Paul. His only purpose was to finish the job. He just wanted to finish what he started—finish His purpose—and get out of there.

> "I have fought a good fight, I have finished my course, I have kept the faith:"
> (2 Timothy 4:7).

Persevere to the End

Paul did not quit. Furthermore, he knew when he finished his assignment. He finished the job and didn't quit. He started it and finished it.

Jesus said that He glorified His Father in the earth and finished what God called Him to do. There are a great many people whom God calls that simply do not finish. Choose today not to be one of those persons.

THE TIMING OF GOD

CHAPTER 22

Finish Strong

Being in the center of the will of God is different for each of us. For many, it may be to join a good dynamic church, get involved in their various ministries, and support it in every way possible. Some people, however, may really think they can't afford that level of commitment. Really? You may not be ready for this, but if you don't give God that level of commitment, you are walking out on Him.

I'm not telling you that you are not going to heaven; I'm saying that you have stepped out of the center of God's will. You must realize that everything known to man is placed in front of good Christians to draw their attention away from the will of God for their lives. The center of God's will is a hard place, not only to attain, but to remain.

Living By Faith

"For which of you, intending to build a tower, sitteth not down first, and counteth the cost, whether he have sufficient to finish it?" (Luke 14:28).

Nora and I were in a faith convention several years ago and a minister said something about living by faith that got the crowd totally excited. All fifteen thousand people were exuberant. I leaned over to Nora and said to her, "I guarantee that there are not 250 people in this entire place that know what they're cheering about." They were of the belief that "living by faith" meant that they were going to drive Cadillacs and wear diamonds. I'm sure that's why they were cheering.

Dr. Jerry Savelle, a prominent teacher and evangelist, teaching on the subject of living by faith, said this, "You know, a lot of people talk about how easy the faith message is. Welcome to faith, welcome to hell." He's right; it can be difficult, but certainly worth it. God said the just shall live by faith. Once you begin your faith journey, you are required to live by faith whether you want to or not. The Bible says that whatever proceeds not from faith is sin. It is much easier to go the way of the world. Nevertheless, whatever you do, don't give up on living in God's plan.

Growing in Faithfulness

The gospel is committed to those who finish what they start. If you've been faithful to finish in the small things, God will make you ruler over much bigger things. On the other hand, if you are prone to quit a task shortly after you start—just because it becomes a bit difficult—you have shown too many character flaws for God to give you the big stuff until you get yourself lined out and spiritually developed.

> Lest haply, after he hath laid the foundation, and is not able to finish it, all that behold it begin to mock him, Saying, This man began to build, and was not able to finish (Luke 14:29-30).

Not finishing your task or assignment is construed as a mockery before the Lord. People look at your situation and laugh at you. They say things like, "I knew Joe wouldn't stay in that Christian thing too long. I knew it. That's the way all those Christians are. They all talk a good game, but they never stay in it. I don't think I want any of it." That individual has a good chance of going to hell because of what Joe did and didn't do. If Joe had remained faithful to what he said, that person may have come a lot closer to getting into the kingdom of God. You must develop what it takes to finish strong. If it gets hard, you get more committed. If it's tough, you get tougher. You may experience a little shipwreck and a few stonings, but that's no big deal. Just finish.

Time for Obedience

> They shall run like mighty men; they shall climb the wall like men of war; and they shall march every one on his ways, and they shall not break their ranks: (Joel 2:7).

God said that this last day army would be an army that would not break ranks. When they are told to advance at all costs to take an enemy position, you won't find them running back to the safety of a trench. They are brave and obedient soldiers who challenge the enemy at every turn and would never think to scatter in every direction from fear. When they are told to take a city, they take the city.

For you, the only thing that matters is to do what God tells you to do, be faithful, and finish your assignment. You must stand against anything and everything designed to discourage you. Far too many people quit, or they follow God only when it's easy, convenient, or when a personal blessing is involved. The world is full of weakness, but let God build strength into you.

When Your Time Comes

There is a time for you to break through and emerge. God will establish you and bring you to the perfect place at the perfect time for a perfect unveiling. Your track record of faithfulness, steadfastness in the face of discouragement, and the ability to finish your God-given assignment is what's imperative for your launch to take place.

There is a time, a season, and a plan. The faithful are finishers, so finish the work. Your next assignment will be waiting.

About the Author

DR. ED KING is the founder and senior pastor of Redemption Church in Knoxville, Tennessee. He also serves as the president of "The Power of the Word" television ministry, which broadcasts to both national and international markets. In addition to these duties, Dr. King has authored eight books to date and traveled to over 60 nations around the world—teaching and preaching the gospel to thousands of people in leadership conferences and evangelistic meetings. He makes his home in Knoxville with his wife and co-pastor, Nora King. Together they have a daughter, Laren, and son, Marcus, who is in heaven.

Power of the Word Ministries
Dr. Ed King
PO Box 52466
Knoxville TN 37950 USA
1.800.956.4433
www.poweroftheword.com
info@poweroftheword.com
youtube.com/user/RedemptionChurch

Redemption Church
3550 Pleasant Ridge Rd
Knoxville TN 37921 USA
865.521.7777
www.redemptionchurch.com
info@redemptionchurch.com
youtube.com/user/RedemptionChurch

Books By Dr. Ed King

 WILL MY PET BE IN HEAVEN?

In this BEST SELLING book, Pastor Ed King gives us a solid, biblical answer about your pet's afterlife. If you or someone you know has lost a pet, you will find great comfort and insight into what the Bible has to say about our beloved animals and their future in heaven.

ISBN: 9781602730687 • 92 pages • Parsons Publishing House

**Available at Redemption Church,
your local bookstore, or online.**

Available at Redemption Church, your local bookstore, or online.

THE TIMING OF GOD

His Timetable for Your Life

In this life-changing book, you will discover the true timetable that God has set up for you at creation. You will see everything in life has a time and a season. God wants to give you remarkable things to experience, but He wants to give them to you when you are ready to handle and enjoy them. After reading and studying this book, you will become more assured than ever that your next move will be by the inspiration and the timing of God.

ISBN: 978160273717 • 118 pages • Parsons Publishing House

LOYALTY
Going Beyond Faithfulness

Pastor Ed King elaborates on the distinctions between faithfulness and loyalty and focuses on lessons learned by looking at the brotherly love of Jonathan and David. Learn how God's grace will meet you to go past faithfulness and enter into loyalty. It all starts with a decision!

ISBN: 9781602730793 • 110 pages • Parsons Publishing House

Available at Redemption Church, your local bookstore, or online.

DEDICATING YOUR HOUSE

Dedicating your house is a rite that every Christian should perform in order to live a quiet and peaceful life. Because you live in your house, you should want and expect God's blessings on it. One way to see those blessings is to thoughtfully and sacredly separate your house for the Lord's work and service. In this book, Dr. King lays out the biblical case for dedicating your house and provides eight easy-to-follow steps.

ISBN: 9781602730861 • 114 pages • Parsons Publishing House

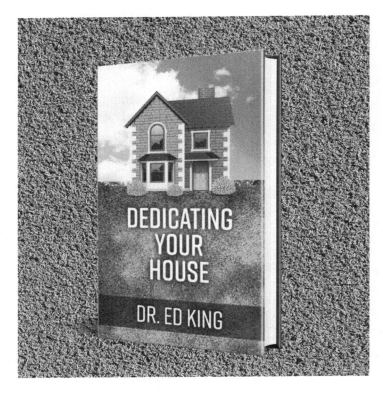

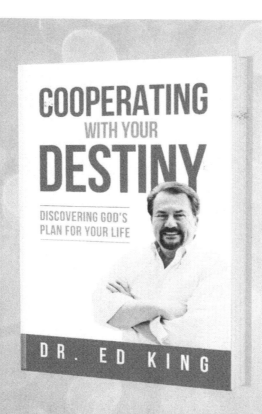

COOPERATING WITH YOUR DESTINY
Discovering God's Plan for Your LIfe

Seeking God's purpose for your life—what He put you on this planet to do—is the most important thing you could ever pursue! God has a good plan for your life that has been designed just for you. Your destiny is a partnership with God orchestrated to cause you to flourish and obtain your eternal reward—all you have to do is join with God's plan!

ISBN: 9781602731349 • 232 pages • Parsons Publishing House

WHAT'S GOING ON?
Why I Believe We Are the Rapture Generation

Although the Bible tells us that no one knows the day or the hour of Jesus' return, God's Word does reveal solid information that illustrates how the signs of the times are lining up for His return to the earth. Pastor Ed King shares insight about the many signs appearing and circumstances playing out at this very hour.

ISBN: 9781973638872 • 298 pages • Westbow Press

Books By Pastor Nora King

30 DAYS TO A BETTER PRAYER LIFE

Nora King offers fresh revelation and practical teaching to help you experience the release of God's power. You will learn daily how to improve your prayer life and enter God's presence through these simple principles. You don't have to struggle in prayer any longer!

ISBN: 9781602730120 • 142 pages • Parsons Publishing House

Trouble May Come, but YOU can RISE above it!

OVERCOMING in DIFFICULT times

Nora King

In these pages, you will discover that with God's help:

- You will get through the storms of life.
- You can resist in times of spiritual attacks.
- You are able to overcome in every battle.

Though we may get knocked down in life, we get up, bounce back and keep going on the journey. If you have been beaten and bruised by the trials of life, whether small or substantial, the truths in this book will help you overcome!

ISBN: 9781602730120 • 142 pages • Parsons Publishing House

Parsons Publishing House
Your Voice Your World ™

AVAILABLE IN BOOKSTORES AND ONLINE

70 REASONS FOR SPEAKING IN TONGUES
Your Own Built in Spiritual Dynamo
by Dr. Bill Hamon
ISBN: 9781602730137 • 216 pages • $14.95 USD.

VOICES—HEARING AND DISCERNING GOD ACCURATELY
by Dr. Robert Gay
ISBN: 9781602731370 • 208 pages • $14.95 USD.

FAITH AFTER FAILURE
Reconnecting with Your Destiny
by Sandie Freed
ISBN: 9781602730557 • 208 pages • $13.95 USD.

WHY DO I DO THE THINGS I DO?
Understanding Personalities
by Dr. Darrell Parsons
ISBN: 9781602730199 • 132 pages • $10.95 USD.

RELEASE YOUR WORDS—IMPACT YOUR WORLD
by Dr. Darrell Parsons
ISBN: 9781602730007 • 140 pages • $9.95 USD.

EMERGING AS AN INNOVATIVE CHRISTIAN LEADER
12 Common Cores for Mobilizing Your Influence into the Future
by Dr. Darrell Parsons
ISBN: 9781602730656 • 228 pages • $14.95 USD.